Start with Gratitude

Reflect, Set Goals, and Live Your Best Year

Date ..../........./.........

"I awoke this morning with devout thanksgiving for my friends, the old and the new."
—Ralph Waldo Emerson

Date ..../........./..........

Date ..../........../..........

Date ..../........./..........

Date ..../........./.........

Date........../........../..........

Date ..../........./.........

Date ..../........./..........

Date ..../........./.........

Date ..../........./..........

Date ..../......../..........

"For me,
every hour is grace.
And I feel gratitude in
my heart each time I can
meet someone and look
at his or her smile."
—Elie Wiesel

Date ..../........./..........

Date........./........./..........

Date ..../........../..........

Date ..../......../........

Date........./........./.........

Date ..../........./..........

"Reflect upon your present blessings—of which every man has many—not on your past misfortunes, of which all men have some."
—Charles Dickens

Date ..../........./.........

Date ..../........./..........

Date ..../........../..........

"Gratitude is a quality similar to electricity: It must be produced and discharged and used up in order to exist at all."
—William Faulkner

Date ..../........./..........

Date ..../........./.........

Date ..../........./..........

Date........./........./..........

Date ..../........../..........

Date ..../........./.........

Date ..../........./..........

"Strive to find things
to be thankful for, and
just look for the good in
who you are."
—Bethany Hamilton

Date ..../........./.........

Date ..../........./..........

Date ..../........./.........

Date ..../........./..........

"Appreciation is
a wonderful thing. It
makes what is excellent
in others belong to us
as well."
—Voltaire

Date........../........../..........

Date ..../........./..........

Date ..../......../........

Date ..../........./..........

Date ..../........./.........

Date ..../........../..........

"When you are grateful, fear disappears and abundance appears."
—Anthony Robbins

Date........./........./.........

"If a fellow
isn't thankful for
what he's got, he isn't
likely to be thankful for
what he's going to get."
—Frank A. Clark

Date ..../........./.........

Date........./........./..........

Date ..../........./..........

"Gratitude
can transform com-
mon days into
thanksgivings, turn routine
jobs into joy, and change
ordinary opportunities into
blessings."
—William Arthur Ward

Date ..../........./.........

Date........./........./..........

Date........./........./..........

Date ..../.........../..........

"Before I get
out of bed, I am
saying thank you. I
know how important it
is to be thankful."
—Al Jarreau

Date ..../........../..........

Date ..../........./.........

Date........./........./..........

Date ..../........./.........

Date ..../........./..........

"Be grateful
in your own hearts.
That suffices.
Thanksgiving has wings,
and flies to its right
destination."
—Victor Hugo

Date........./........./.........

Date ..../........./..........

Date........./........./.........

"A thankful heart is not only the greatest virtue, but the parent of all the other virtues."
—Cicero

Date ..../........./.........

Date ..../.........../...........

Date ..../........../..........

Date........./........./.........

Date ..../........./..........

"I would
maintain that
thanks are the highest
form of thought; and that
gratitude is happiness
doubled by wonder."
—G.K. Chesterton

Date........./........./.........

Date........./........./..........

Date ..../.........../..........

"Acknowledging the good that you already have in your life is the foundation for all abundance."
—Eckhart Tolle

Date ..../........./..........

Date ..../........./..........

Date ..../........./..........

Date........./........./..........

Date ..../.........../..........

"When eating fruit,
remember the one
who planted
the tree."
—Vietnamese
Proverb

Date ..../........./.........

"He is a wise man who does not grieve for the things which he has not, but rejoices for those which he has."
—Epictetus

Date ..../........./.........

Date........./........./..........

Date........./........./..........

Date........./........./.........

Date ..../........../..........

Date ..../........./..........

"When I started counting my blessings, my whole life turned around."
—Willie Nelson

Date ..../........../..........

Date ..../......../..........

"Silent
gratitude isn't very
much to anyone."
—Gertrude Stein

Date........../........../..........

Date ..../........./.........

Date ..../........./..........

Date........../........../..........

Date ..../........./.........

Date........../........../..........

"One can
never pay in
gratitude; one can only
pay 'in kind' somewhere
else in life."
—Anne Morrow
Lindbergh

Date ..../........./.........

Date ..../........./..........

Date........./........./.........

"This a
wonderful day. I've
never seen this one
before."
—Maya Angelou

Date ..../........./..........

Date........./........./..........

Date ..../......../..........

Date........./........./..........

Date........../........../..........

Date ..../........./..........

Date ..../......../..........

"Enjoy the
little things, for one
day you may look back
and realize they were the
big things."
—Robert Brault

Date........./........./..........

Date ..../........../..........

Look for more Gratitude Journals in this special series to come soon.

Published by Citation Media LLC
citationmedia1@gmail.com

Author: C. Marie
ISBN-10: 1-7341429-1-X
ISBN-13: 978-1-7341429-1-4
Copyright 2020 Citation Media LLC